Table of Contents

Aa 2-3	Shape Up Those Numbers 56
Bb 4-5	Play Ball with These Numbers 57
Cc 6-7	Today Is the Day 58
Dd 8-9	Moving Through The Months 59
Ee 10-11	Memorable Months 60
Ff 12-13	Directing Directions 61
Gg 14-15	Connecting Compounds 62
Hh 16-17	Attracting Opposites 63
Ii 18-19	Action Everyone! 64
Jj 20-21	Bear-able Friends 65
Kk 22-23	Pizza with Pizazz 66
Ll 24-25	Hot Dog Perfection 67
Mm 26-27	Circus Action 68
Nn 28-29	Fantastic Flavors for All 69
Oo 30-31	Topsy-Turvy T-Shirts 70
Pp 32-33	A World of Languages 71
Qq 34-35	A Perfect Place 72
Rr 36-37	It's a Date! 73
Ss 38-39	They Just Belong Together ... 74
Tt 40-41	Cooling Off 75
Uu 42-43	Make a Sentence 76
Vv 44-45	Time and Money 77
Ww 46-47	Compared to You 78
Xx 48-49	Saving Up! 79
Yy 50-51	Nutty Escapades 80
Zz 52-53	
Countdown for School 54	
Order a Number of These 55	

IF0185 Modern Manuscript   ©1992 Instructional Fair, Inc.

Aa

AA

aa

Aa

Arizona

Albert

Alice

airplane

ant

aviator

Aa

Ants accept award.

Active ants applaud.

Annie ate apples.

Bb

Bb

bb

Bb

Brazil

Bernie

Betsy

bear

bubble

bath

Cc

Cc

cc

Cc

Canada

Charlie

Claire

cow

candy

cat

Dd

DD

dd

Dd

Dallas

Dwayne

Denise

dolphins

dance

draw

D d

Daisy dunks donuts.

Ducks draw dogs.

Dolphins dive deep.

Ee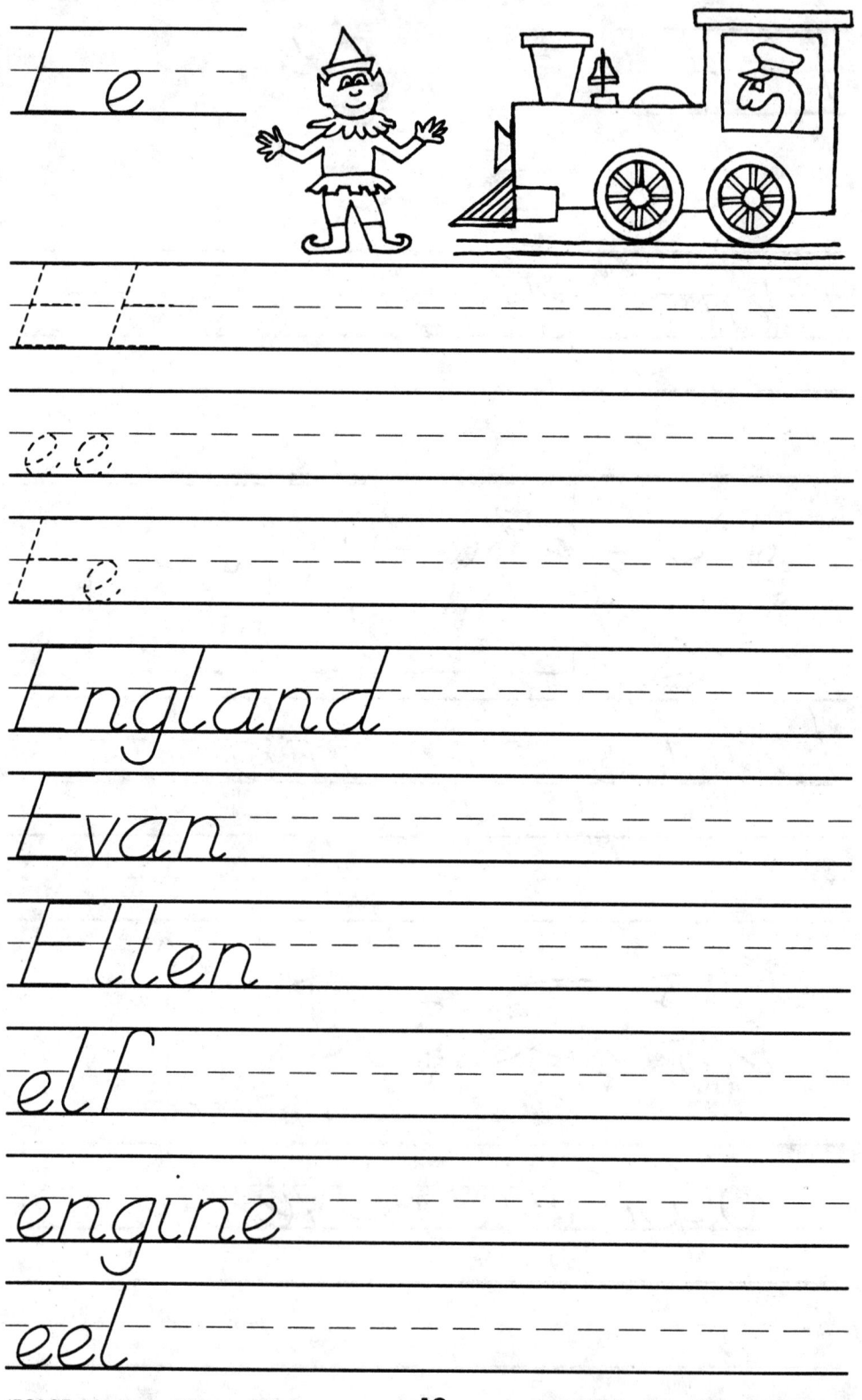

E

e

Ee

England

Evan

Ellen

elf

engine

eel

Ee

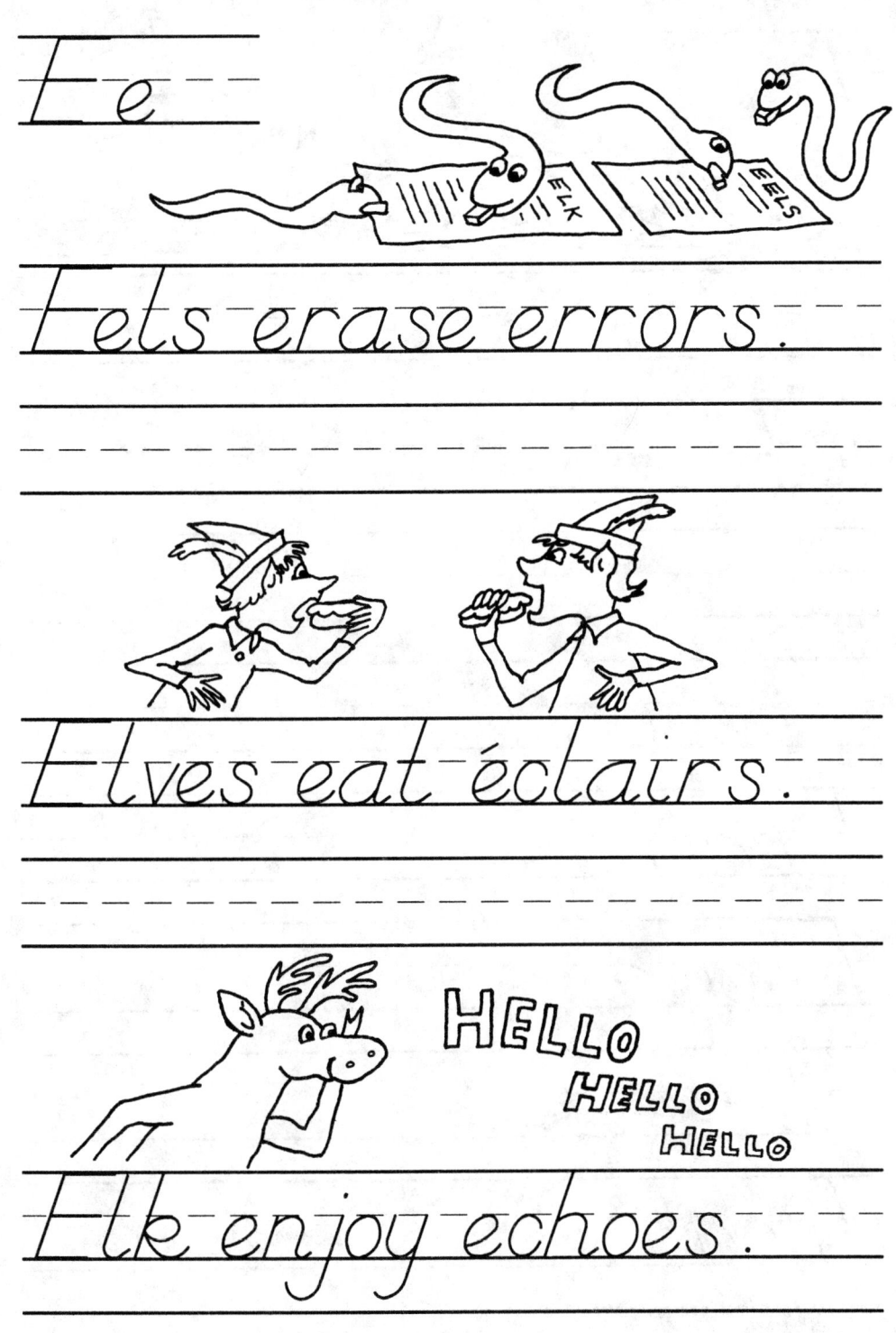

Eels erase errors.

Elves eat éclairs.

Elk enjoy echoes.

Ff

ff

Ff

Freeport

Frank

Fiona

fly

frog

find

Gg

Gg

gg

Gg

Germany

Greg

Glenda

goggles

garden

goat

Gg

Gophers golf.

Goat grows grapes.

Geese gather grain.

Houston

Henry

Helen

horse

hippo

hike

Hh

Hippo hangs hats.

Horses hide horns.

Hogs haul hay.

Ii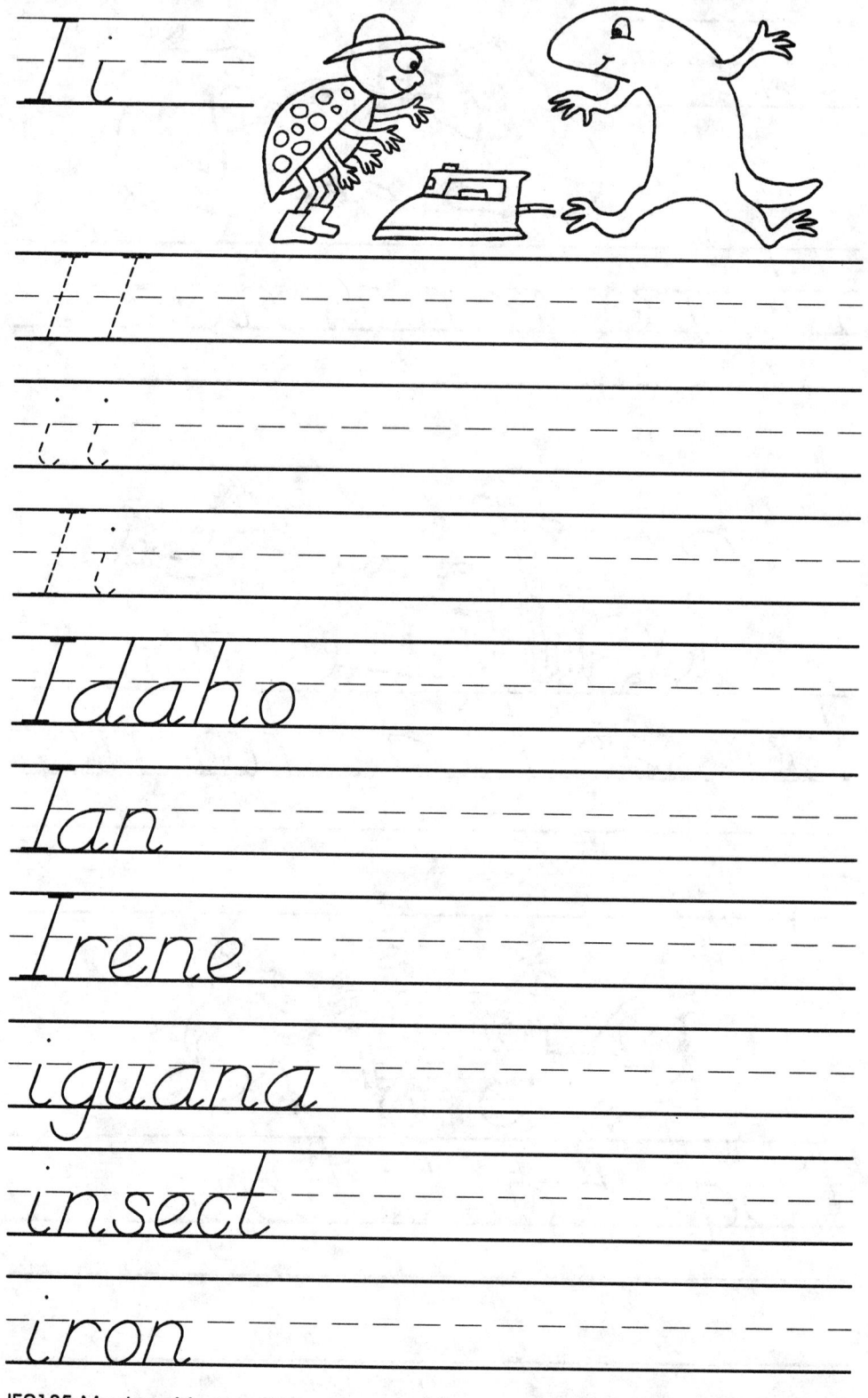

Ii

Ii

Ii

Idaho

Ian

Irene

iguana

insect

iron

Ii

Ida irons ivy.

Inchworms itch.

Insects inspect ice.

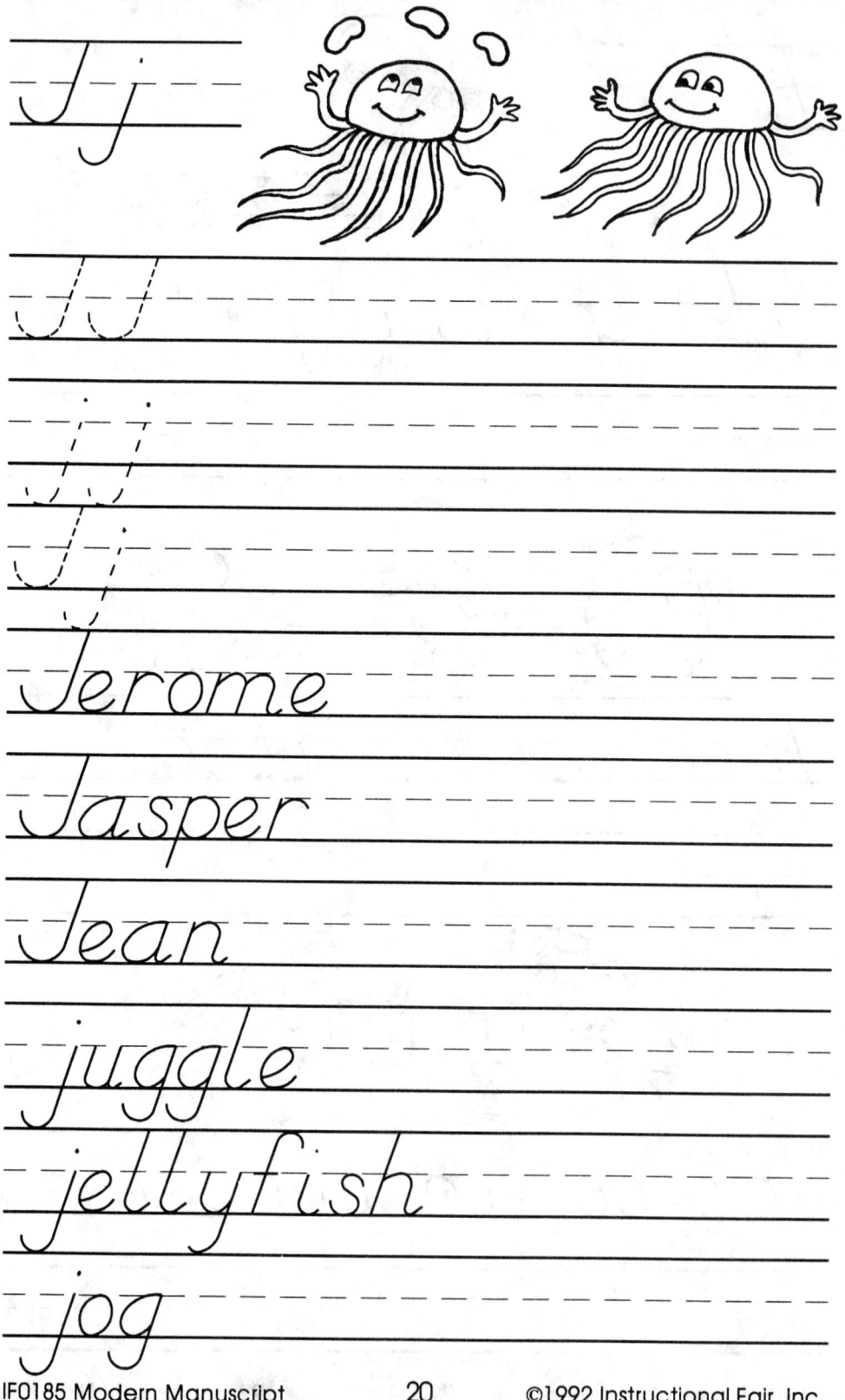

Jj

Jj

jj

jj

Jerome

Jasper

Jean

juggle

jellyfish

jog

Jj

Jolly joggers jiggle.

Jellyfish judge jam.

Jaguars juggle jets.

K k

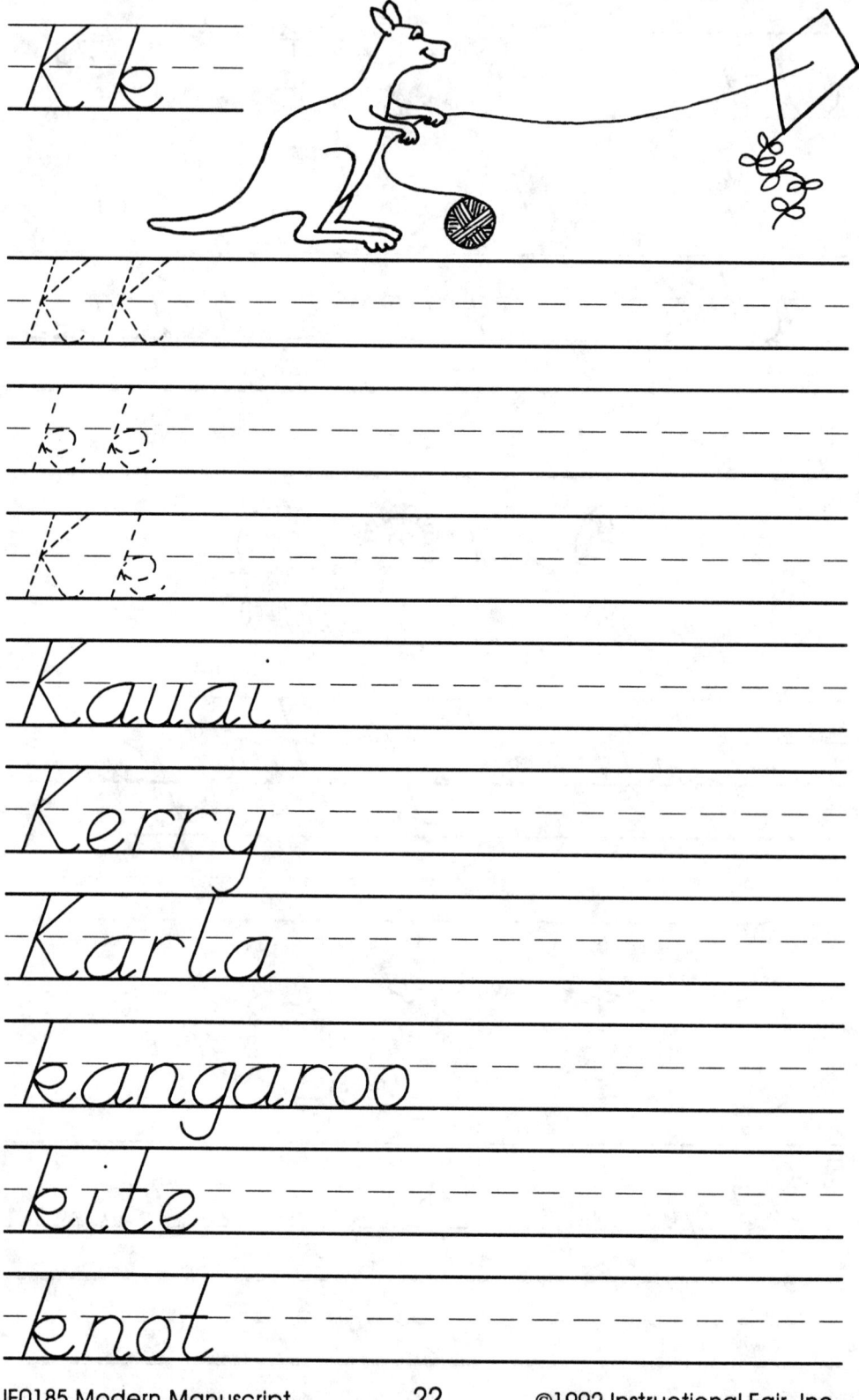

K K

k k

K k

Kauai

Kerry

Karla

kangaroo

kite

knot

K k

Koalas kiss kids.

Kangaroos kick.

Kings knit kilts.

Ll

Ll

Ll

Ll

Longview

Lionel

Lucy

lion

ladders

like

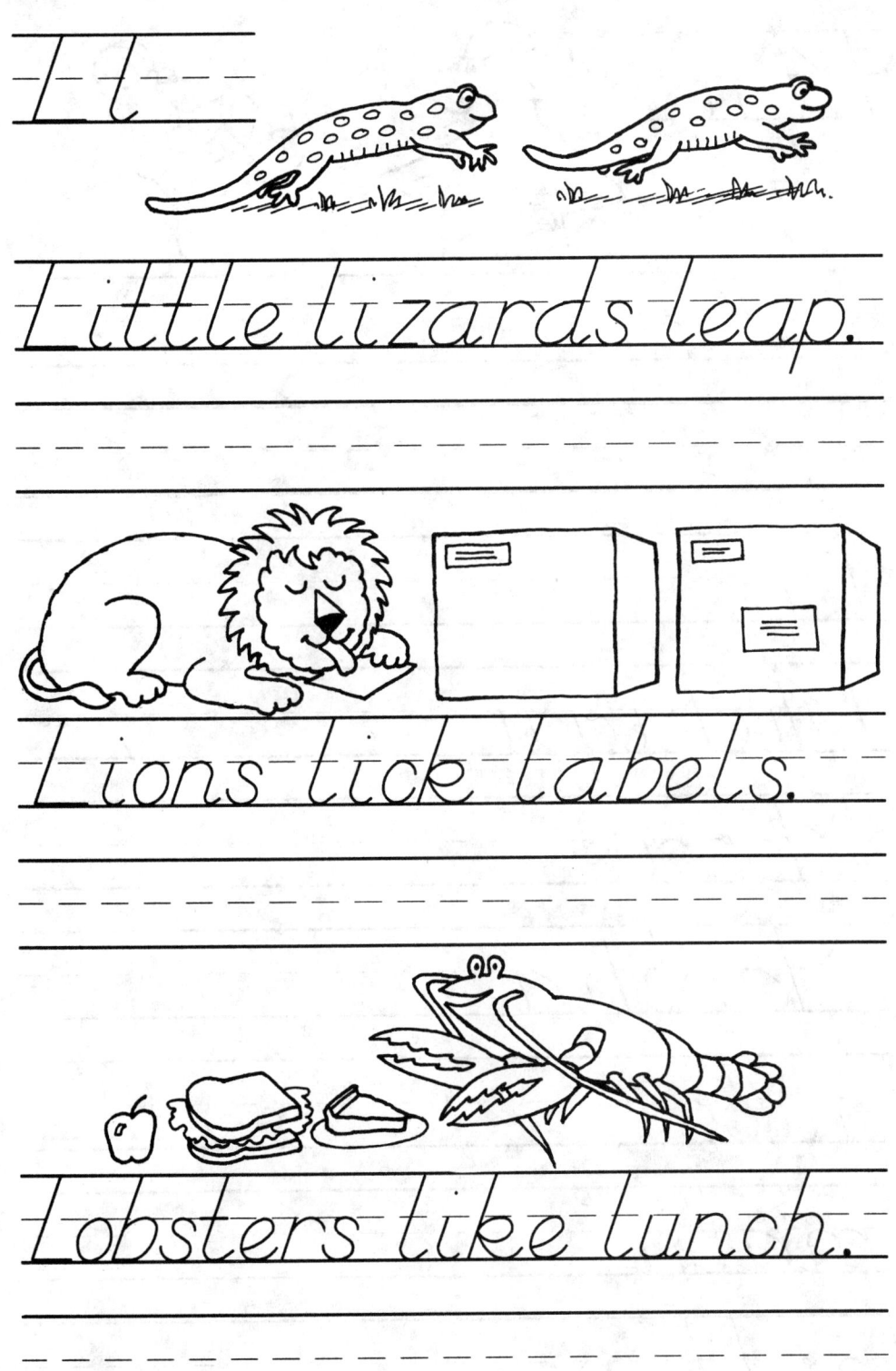

Ll

Little lizards leap.

Lions lick labels.

Lobsters like lunch.

Mm

Mike molds mugs.

Mules make mitts.

Mice mend mittens.

Nn

Nina nibbles nuts.

Ned numbers notes.

Newts need nets.

Oahu

Ollie

Olivia

oyster

orange

otter

Oo

Oxen order omelets.

Otters oil ovens.

Owls obey orders.

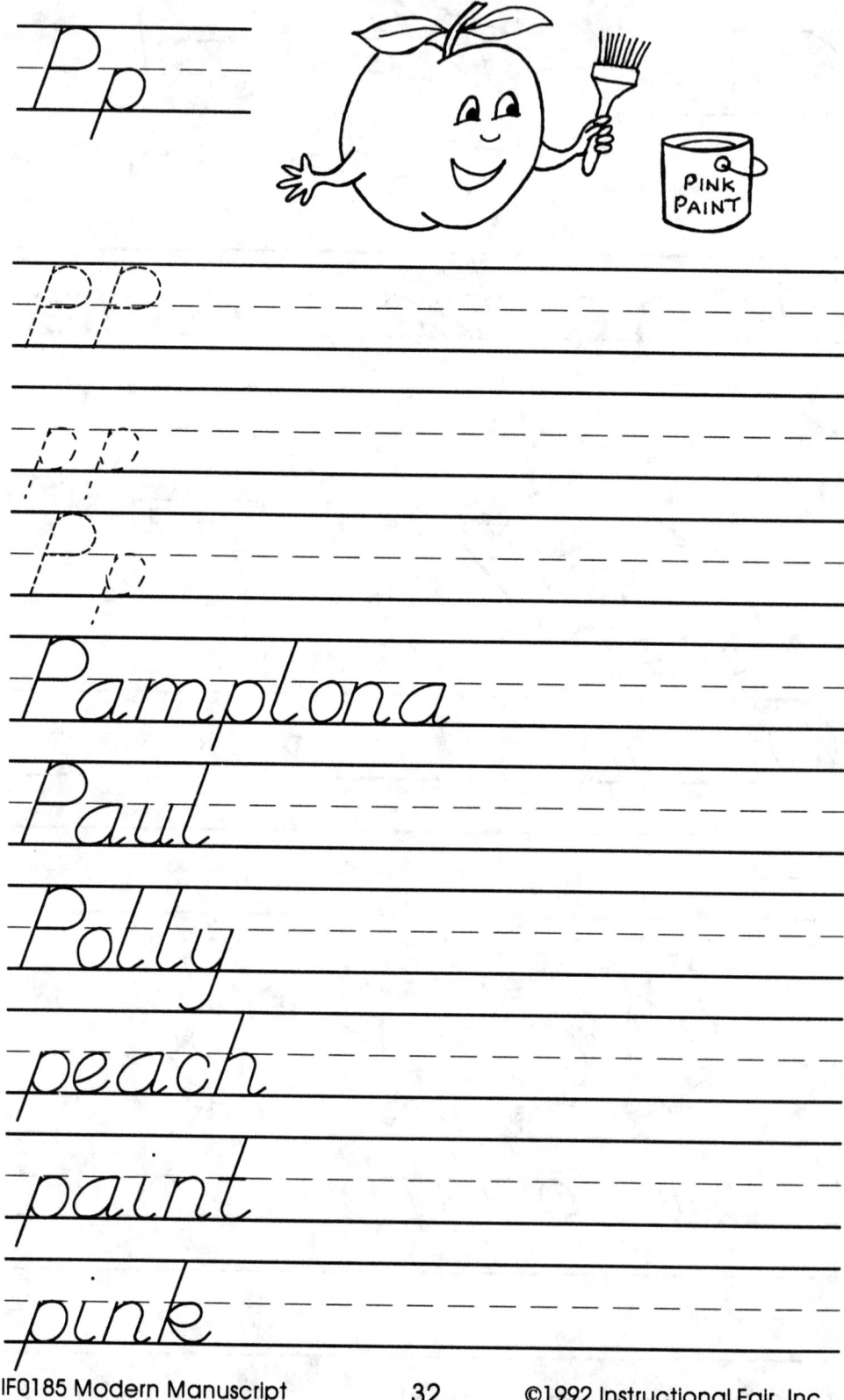

Pp

Pp

Pp

Pp

Pamplona

Paul

Polly

peach

paint

pink

Pp

Pigs poke presents.

Polly plays pianos.

Pats pat pizzas.

Qq

Quilts quiver.

Quails quilt.

Quincy quacks.

Rr

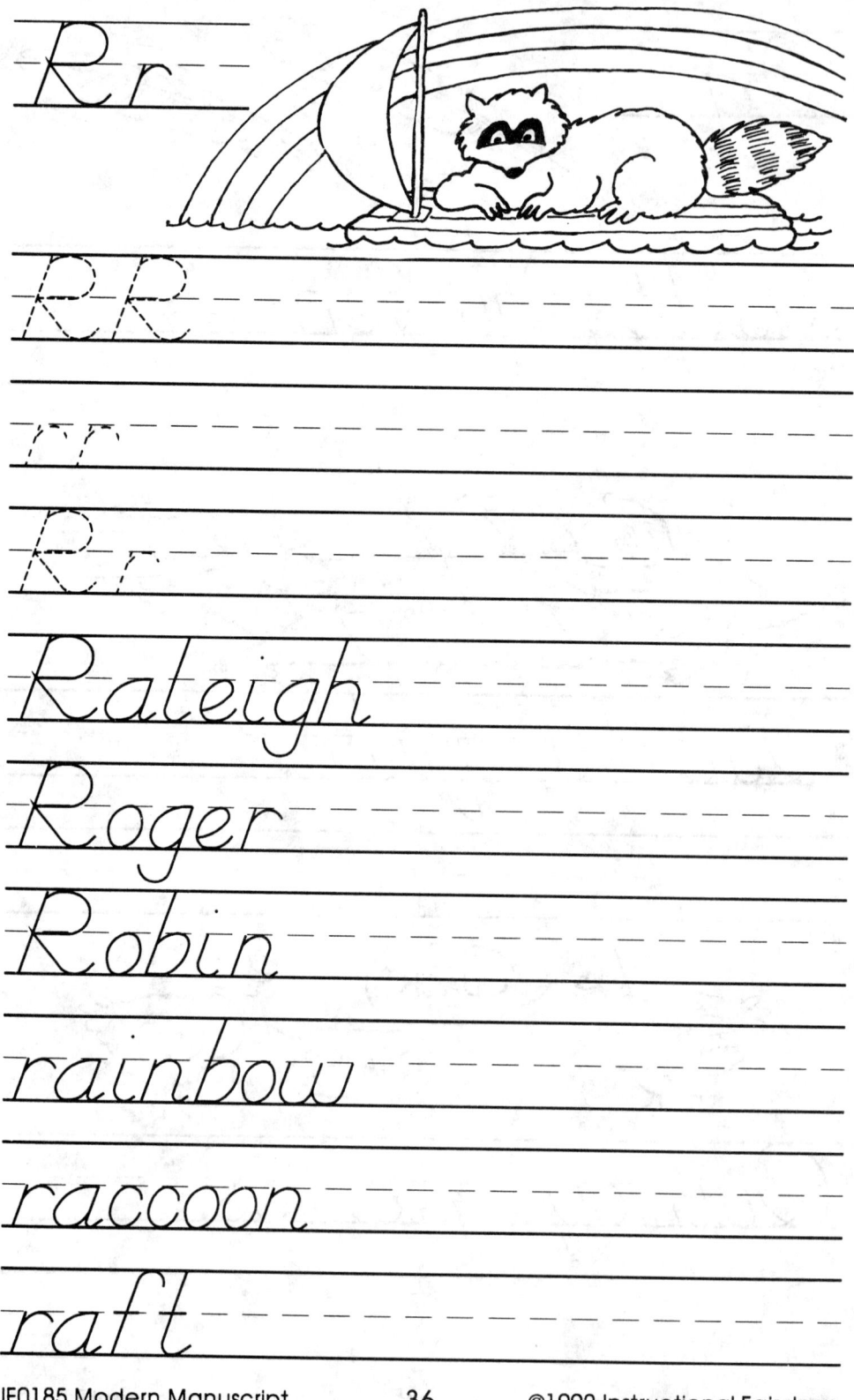

RR

rr

Rr

Raleigh

Roger

Robin

rainbow

raccoon

raft

Ss

Ss

Ss

Ss

Seville

Simon

Susan

star

soap

smile

Ss

Seahorses surf.

Stars shine ships.

Seals sell skates.

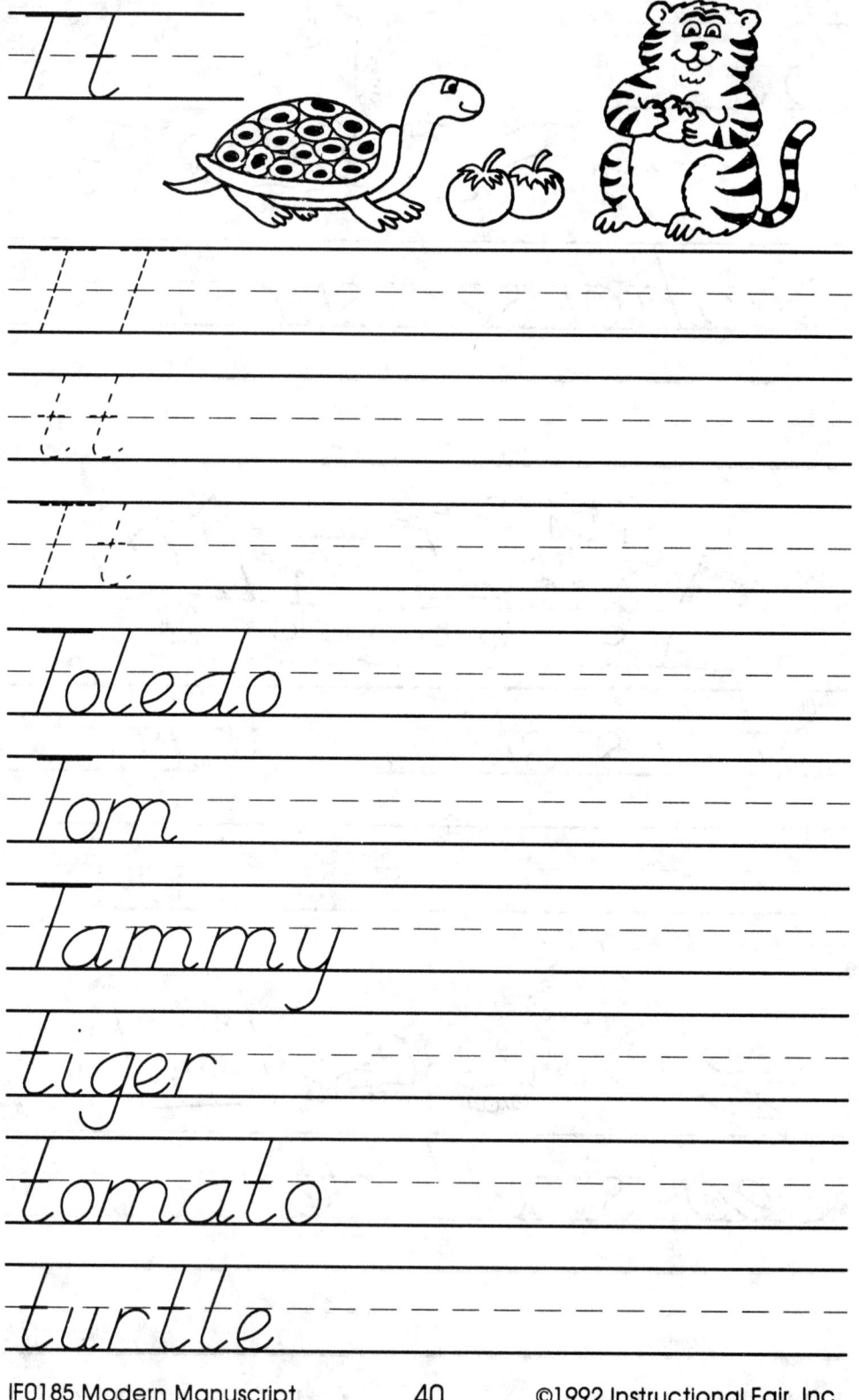

Tt

Tt

tt

tt

Toledo

Tom

Tammy

tiger

tomato

turtle

Tt

Turtles toot tubas.

Toad times trains.

Tigers take taxis.

Uu

Uu

uu

Uu

Uruguay

Uri

Unice

unicorn

umbrella

usual

Uu

Uri urges unicorns.

Unice unpacks urns.

Umps use uniforms.

Venice

Vance

Vera

vacuum

violets

view

Vv

Viola views vests.

Vera visits villages.

Van vacuums vats.

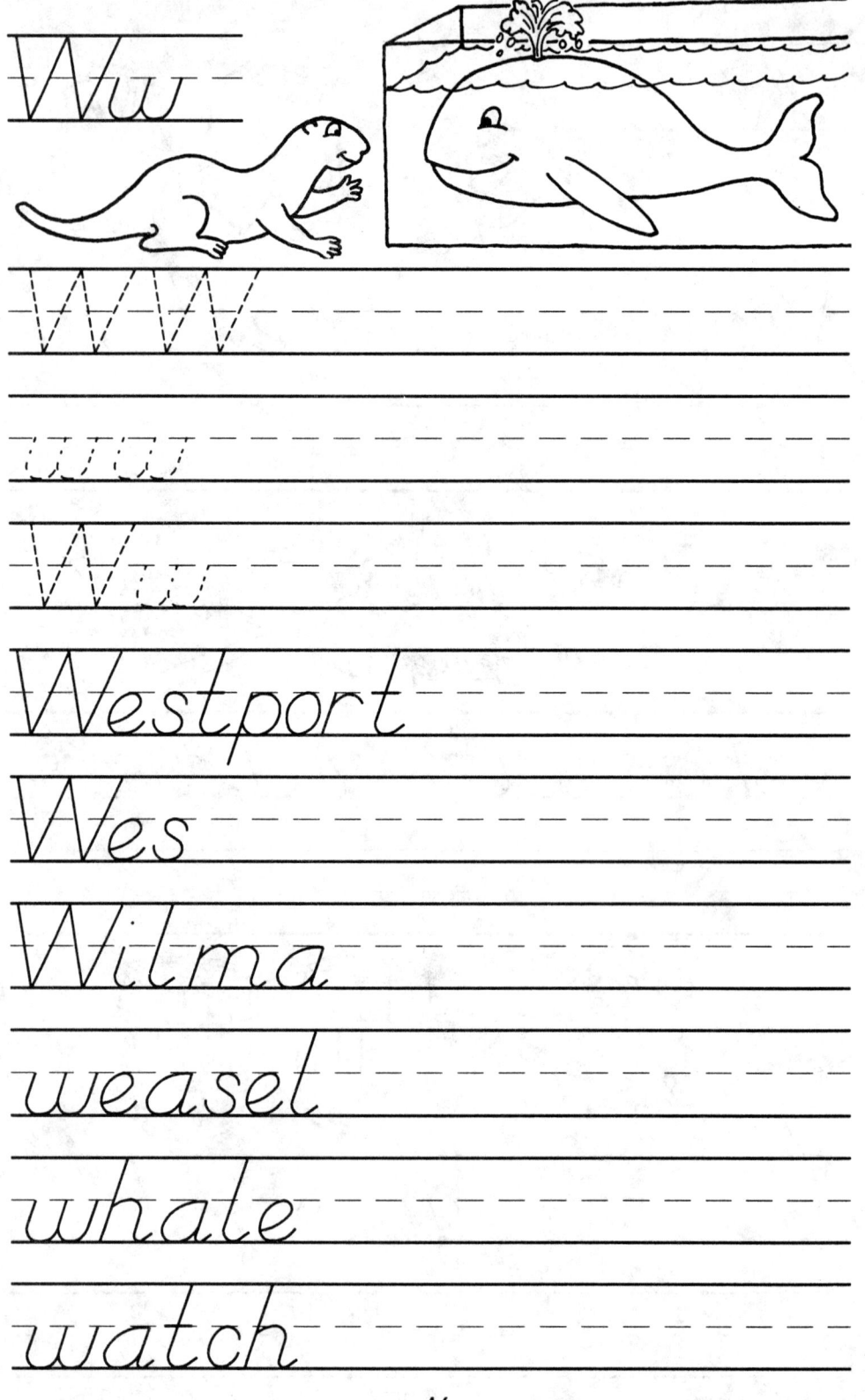

Ww
ww
ww
Ww

Westport
Wes
Wilma
weasel
whale
watch

Ww

Wes waxes wheels.

Ward wants wind.

Whales wiggle.

Xx

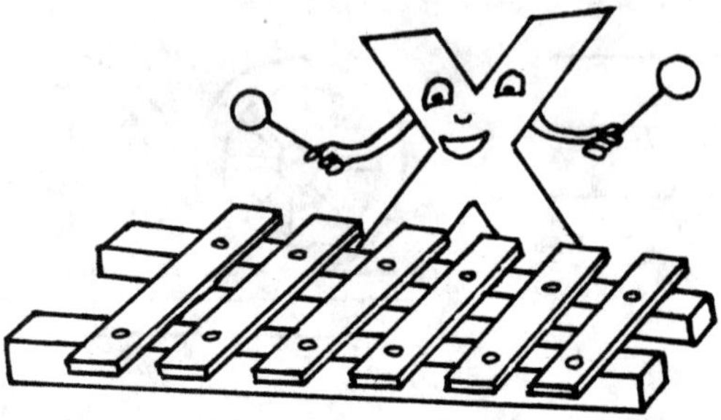

Xx

Xx

Xx

Xenia

Xavier

Xina

xylophone

x-ray

Xmas

Xx x-rays xylophones.

Xavier x's x-rays.

Xina x'd Xeroxes.

Yy

Yy

yy

Yucatan

Yolanda

Yvonne

yo-yo

yarn

yes

Yy

Yvette yawns.

Yaks yell, "Yeah!"

Yvonne yanks yarn.

Zeeland

Zeb

Zelda

zoom

zipper

zebra

Zz

Zippers zip.

Zebras zigzag.

Zookeepers zoom.

Countdown for School

Color, trace and write.

1 one

2 two

3 three

4 four

5 five

Order a Number of These

Color, trace and write.

6 six

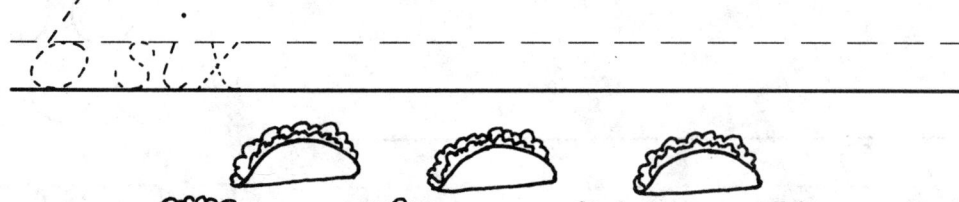

7 seven

8 eight

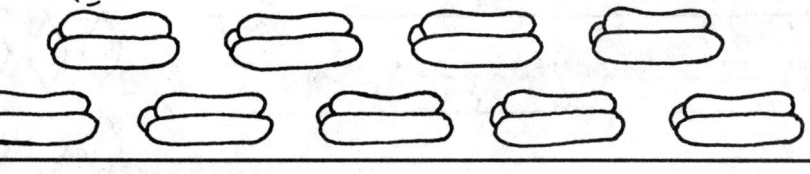

9 nine

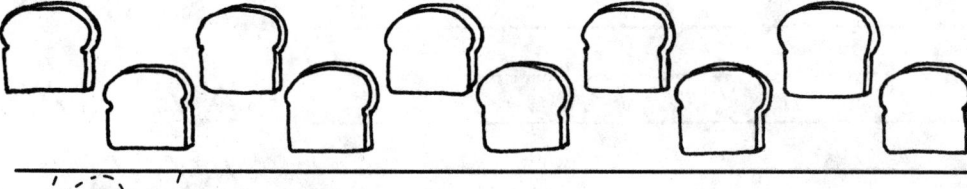

10 ten

Shape Up Those Numbers

Color, trace and write.

11 eleven

12 twelve

13 thirteen

14 fourteen

15 fifteen

Play Ball with These Numbers

Color, trace and write.

16 sixteen

17 seventeen

18 eighteen

19 nineteen

20 twenty

Today Is the Day

Trace and write.

Sunday

Monday

Tuesday

Wednesday

Thursday

Friday

Saturday

Moving Through the Months

Color, trace and write.

January

February

March

April

May

June

Memorable Months

Color, trace and write.

July

August

September

October

November

December

Directing Directions

Trace and write.

up

down

right

left

over

under

off

on

in

Connecting Compounds

Draw a line to match the two words that make a compound word. Then write each compound word on the line.

back	side
in	pack
every	where
barn	yard

rain	keeper
zoo	bow
foot	eater
ant	ball

Attracting Opposites

Draw a line to match the two words that mean the opposite. Then write both words on the line.

stop	dark
light	go
big	wet
dry	little

open	off
on	play
high	close
work	low

Action Everyone!

Write the words where they belong.

Hint:
Nouns name people, places and things.
Verbs show action.

playground   draw   shout   book   jog
puppy   library   sing   eat   boy
desk   read   girl   see

Nouns   **Verbs**

Bear-able Friends

Write the names of the different kinds of bears beginning with your favorite.

1. -

2. -

3. -

4. -

5. -

6. -

Pizza with Pizzazz!

Write six ingredients you would use to make your own pizza.

crust olives
cheese onions
sausage mushrooms
pepperoni ham
green peppers Canadian bacon
tomato sauce

1. _____
2. _____
3. _____
4. _____
5. _____
6. _____

Hot Dog Perfection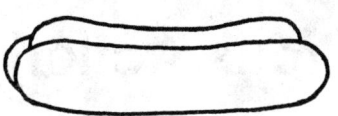

Write the hot dog toppings beginning with your favorite.

| ketchup | mustard | sauerkraut | cheese |
| pickles | onions | tomatoes | chili |

1. _____

2. _____

3. _____

4. _____

5. _____

6. _____

7. _____

8. _____

9. _____

Circus Action

Write the circus acts in alphabetical order.

jugglers   clowns   highwire
trapeze   lions   elephants
bears   acrobats

1. ----------------------------
2. ----------------------------
3. ----------------------------
4. ----------------------------
5. ----------------------------
6. ----------------------------
7. ----------------------------
8. ----------------------------

Fantastic Flavors for All

Write the jellybean flavors in alphabetical order.

watermelon   lemon   cinnamon
orange   grape   mint
strawberry   tangerine

1. _____
2. _____
3. _____
4. _____
5. _____
6. _____
7. _____
8. _____

Topsy-Turvy T-Shirts

Write the word that tells about the picture on the T-shirt.

sail
read
paint
surf
skateboard
bicycle
jog

1.

2.

3.

4.

5.

6.

7.

A World of Languages

Draw a line to match the country to its language. Then write both words on the line.

England	Spanish	China	Chinese
France	English	Italy	Swedish
Germany	French	Norway	Norwegian
Spain	German	Sweden	Italian

A Perfect Place

Copy the sentences on the lines

Foxy sees an open door.

She pushes it open to look inside.

She curls up on the rug for a nap.

It's a Date!

Write the sentences correctly. Use capital letters and periods where they belong.

valentine's day is on february 14th

st patrick's day is on march 17th

new year's day is on january 1st

They Just Belong Together

Write the two words that go together. Write the word **and** between them.

needle	eggs	shirt	thread
water	bacon	pencil	butter
meatballs	bread	soap	dry
spaghetti	tie	wash	paper

Cooling Off

How do you like to cool off on a hot summer day?

drink lemonade
run in sprinklers
eat ice cream
sail my boat
go to the beach
sit by a fan
swim slowly
water ski

Make a Sentence

Combine words from each list to make complete sentences. Then write the sentences on the lines.

List 1	List 2	List 3
They	galloped	to the river.
Two kittens	slept	under the blanket.
A zebra	jumped	in the puddles.

1.

2.

3.

Time and Money

Write the words where they belong.

cents   penny   dollar   nickel
half-dollar dime   minute   week
year   month   second
day   quarter   hour

Time Words   **Money Words**

Compared to You

Write each word where it belongs to tell if it is taller or shorter than you.

ant   plane   door
desk   dinosaur   flower
wagon   flagpole   dragonfly
kitten   ruler   skyscraper
house   giraffe

Shorter   **Taller**

Saving Up!

Unscramble the words in each bank to make a sentence. Write each sentence correctly on the lines.

1. money in his puts bank. the Mike
2. of all money. He his saves
3. will a bike. for enough Soon he have

1.

2.

3.

Nutty Escapades

Unscramble the words in each acorn to make a sentence. Write each sentence correctly on the lines.

1. saw of Squirrel lots acorns.
2. scurried the He down tree.
3. He ran the nuts and up the tree. gathered

1.

2.

3.